HALF-CENTURY STATUS

A. RAZOR

Words As Works Publishing

Half -Century Status
A. Razor

ISBN-13: 978-0615792163

ISBN-10: 0615792162

©A. Razor

Word As Works Publishing

c/o :
Punk Hostage Press
P.O. Box 1869
Hollywood CA
90078

Introduction

I am fifty years-old this year, 2013. I am most grateful to have lived this long and to have been around this place for all the things I have seen and done. This is a collection of poems that came to me in truncated form, much like "status updates" on the social media of our modern times.

I could decry all the evils of the internet, what it has done to books, music and art in general, or I could sing its praises. I will do neither here. It has done what it has done and it is doing what it is doing. It is for those who are about to eclipse me in the next several decades to really understand and decide what all of that will mean. I merely just want to tip my hat to the times, as well as the previous forty-nine years that preceded this one, in order to celebrate with a little of the music that makes the dance possible.

So, here it is, for you, in gratitude, for your support and your acknowledgement. I hope these words give a tickle where they should and a feeling where it is needed. I hope that the money spent on this book furthers the work of so many writers that have come together over the years in my presence and the many that will continue to come together in the many hopeful years to come. May you find a blessing here, or a shelter, or even a home, if possible, while you travel on through the cosmos and we keep reading all these words together.

Peace,

A. Razor   2013

Many thanks to everyone who has ever read something I wrote and liked it enough to have it mean something to you.

Much love to you all.

'never hate a hustle, just hate being hustled enough to never hustle yourself'

-

A. Razor

1.

she says she loves me
but the house is a mess

words can't begin to say
what I would do for the
chance
to just let us both be free
of all the hell that binds us
& let this blood roll forever
like it was never meant to be
held back for nothing ever again

2.

people are in awe of the power
as the prince walks through the province

perhaps that was not so powerful
as rocks & stones resemble gods
that once trampled the greatest man
as we scampered among the crags of time

the death that comes reveals no warrant
for peace
only a purpose of pretense in a political
smile
& there are jobs that are done
& then there are works that are created
& then there is this mangled pile of bodies
underneath the footfalls of the fearful
mighty

3.

all wound up
ready to spin
so we can
now begin
then

4.

tearing up the road like it was yesterday
all along the way screaming out the
windows
howling at the moon, each exhaled breath
 a foggy burst
this is how souls feel on fire at high speeds,
drowning
on the oxygen that once gave them a
normalcy in breathing
that was too good to be true in moments
before intuition
begets all the fatal applause of the
 loneliness choir
when the moon passes under the clouds
then
 you realize that no one is driving
as you look at your hands
with the disbelief
that they ever drove anything anywhere,
least of all crazy

5.

way past midnight on a shitty deal
walking away from the table empty
these are the reasons we are not
reasonable
now that the scars are on the inside
the ghost of what never gets born
lingers the longest in the air
this time of night
this time of morning
this time

6.

what people seem to be forgetting
is that it wasn't a car park
when they buried the body
of the lost & crippled king
to hide the disgrace of empire

what people might want to consider
is where their bones might end up
1,000 years from now
depending on what crowns they lose
what battles were fought
what betrayals there were
with no one ever knowing
what hearts must have been broken
without the words of hapless bards
in trouble with the king's laws

7.

when you have been there so many times
gun barrels to your head & to your back
laying face down, kicks & punches
coming onto your body, so numb
wrists twisted in the metal clamp
unable to fight back anymore
you forget that most folks
think it will never happen
to them in this lifetime
until they pay attention
to what laws are coming into play
how the books are getting stacked
against them
how unnecessary they have already become
in the rich new world of shelving filled with
boxes
made up of so many colors of the rainbow
so pretty so beautiful, if you cannot afford
to buy some more of it now, then you might
be marked for the labor camps soon
as they are already watching us making
our way
from the eyes of drones on high
as we plod along toward the slow motion
meat grinder
we helped build as a monument
to modern progress
only to realize we were all the meat it
needed
after it was already too late

8.

I am in & out
like the blade
I am through
& through
like the
bullet
in the
master shot
I am ready to blow
like the hand grenade
with the pin just pulled

9.

In the hospital
Before work
Begins
Wondering
How much longer
It would be
Before the need
To come here
Will happen again
So maybe I can
Forget my own
Mortality
A little while longer

10.

sometimes you can feel the meteors come
closer
traveling somewhere in the unseen outer
space
while you are wishing all your words were
worthy
of being chiseled in stone sculptures
instead of just lights sent out into the ether
on some soft collision course that knows no
destiny

11.

temptation is waiting
for everyone out there
in little drops of desire
that trickle constantly
inside our collective minds
no matter what head dress
we are anointed with
by human gods or
birds of prey

12.

she asked, quixotically
'why don't you fix
all of the typos
in your book
yet, you work so hard
to make other writer's books
so perfect?'
I reply, earnestly,
emphatically,
'I am not done
writing any books
of my own, yet.'

13.

just a job
lives in
the balance

broken, interrupted
lives, barely living
barely worth much
by society's standards

but, when you look
into their eyes
no matter the age
no matter the journey
that brought them to
the doorstep of
your job

they are all lives
worth saving
they are all lives,
nonetheless

14.

the president's men asked me if
I had the president's back
before he gave the
State of the Union
address
I stuttered to find
an answer
or a reply
until I realized
they were not
actually
speaking to me

15.

as the morning fog clears
love seems restless
holidays that become uncertain
toss & turn all night
just to see the dawn
obscured by slight weather
the moments before
someone is there
upon awakening
as the horn warns the ships
way off in the unseen distance
as they might be in danger of
coming too close to the point
before the last of the fog clears

16.

missing the bus
on a Sunday
afternoon
in Point Richmond
means waiting an hour
for the next bus to come

it means sitting there with
your whole life behind you
with what's left of it
in front of you
while the refinery billows smoke
on the other side of the freeway
as dogs chase tennis balls thrown
by nervous dog owners while pelicans
fly overhead toward the bay

an hour of this
to see where
you are at
knowing
luck has
nothing
to do
with it
anymore

17.

when the man that showed us
how to play tag, your it
dies in his sleep
there is no
power
left
for
us
if we are to be true to our hearts
if we are to stop playing around
in such a way that leaves us empty
as rain drops run jagged pathways
down iron tinted widows looking out
on gray skies, dark clouds, bare branches
that are
bending so slightly away from where we
once were before

18.

Underneath a downpour
Of stale air & love
Choking for forgiveness
There is a child
Always hopeful
She may see
Her Poppa
Again

19.

art is stolen
off of lips
of those who
speak it
as it was
created
long before
those who have
seen it, heard it, felt it, tasted it

taken from the minds of those
who never even knew it existed

it was created before
it was experienced
it was experience
before it was created

20.

the sun

waiting all night
for an unknown
delivery
that never came
until just now

the sun

21.

peanut butter might have saved the world
if it had not somehow led to the
overpopulation
that caused all the jelly to spread out in the
ocean
looking for the source of all the fishiness
that was about
to swim off into the deepest trench of
hidden treasure
among the lost stars that are lying
                              below
                              the surface

22.

late night wandering
picking flowers
under cover
of darkness

fingertips covered in fragrant tones
that emit colors & emotions with
each breath taken in, memories
jarred with every aroma as it
hits home inside their head
takes roots inside the mind

the racket & bell ringing
of the approaching train
slowly pounding
down the tracks toward us
breaks the covert trance we
have been seduced into
by the warming smell
of springtime around
the next corner

the moon is receding slowly
so we mimic it in long strides
massive bunches of cuttings
taken in dimly lit back streets
they are alive with the smell
that will be turned into new
bouquets of color & incense
upon our arrival home

23.

sand in the axle grease
glass shards in the snow
teardrops in the half n' half
bullets on the nightstand
all you need is one
to end the run
of champions

24.

The little parts of the world
That take all night
In silent slow motion
Only make us lose
Our place
For a moment
Then the sun rises again

25.

the dirt farmer took the st. francis nap
as ma bell, southern bell & pac bell
could no longer ring for room service
as the bell huey newton helicopter ride
went blazing off into the sunset saddle
with M-60 machine guns all along the I-80
corridor
where drones pray & reap away in grand
filibuster
traditions of hymnal speechwriters taking
out new app ads
as the mickey mouse club foot kids
sang acapella autotune anthems
for the soldiers that went rape nuts
in the last bit of art official forest left
on the brighter side of a darkened moon
that had lonely footprints marking a slow
start in an arms race with no legs
that had great expectations
only to fall short of the finishing school line
before the easiest lesson was ever learned

26.

Talking down the suicide
From a bed sheet noose
In the shower stall
Lost & Found along the rounds
This moment can pass
If you let it
This moment doesn't
Have to be the end
He looks at me
Like he is uncertain
Whether or not
To thank me
Or just never trust me
Ever again

27.

lemons in the tree
love on the mind
artichokes in the belly
apocalypse in the dreams

28.

pull the ripcord
on your heart
let the words
come forth
so true

29.

lukewarm coffee, tepid tea
find out who really loves me
with opens eyes that now can see

30.

she digs other dudes
more than her old man
he is just a disaster
waiting
to reoccur
so it just seems natural
to have a good time
with other folks
that is why they
call it
making sense
instead of
making love

31.

if you take all the toys from the sandbox
even if they were there before you came
& played with them
claiming them as yours
now crying that you were slighted
for not getting your way
for not being given
someone else's laurels
to sit upon, rest upon
how can you ever hope
to get cleaned up
looking skyward
seeing clear skies
no chance for rain?

32.

running all night long back then, so young
stab wounds were like scraped knees,
youth healed into scars that felt good
for all the while you could run out into it
dusted, coked out, drunken spitting up
demons like contradictions about a world
you wanted to change, but it was changing
you
more than you could stand, feeling like the
mid-west must have felt during the last ice
age, so pressed down from it all, crushed
down, like you knew you would be wide
open plains for ever, good for nothing but
growing grass & collecting piles of buffalo
dung

33.

just below the ancient paving stones
lay all the secrets of the past
ending at the dilapidated docks
where the ocean crushes artifice
against all the jagged rocks
grinding it all down into granular arrays
to mingle it with the eternal sands of time

34.

moon in the sky tonight
looking like a clipped fingernail
a faint slivering of hope

35.

a cold piece of work
with a big heart
beauty forever
life in the eyes
that is deeper
than the days
it takes
to get
from
here
to
the
sun
& back
again
that is the only way
to even begin
to measure this love

36.

in what was caste out
as ugly & unwanted
by the ruling mob
I found a beauty
that is seldom seen
in glimpses so brief
yet, so stunning
they will be the last thing
I think of before I die

37.

the boxer that lays down
is no longer a boxer
how the fight
can end that way
there is no way to imagine
what a beating that must be
what suffering comes from surrender
when it is done in secrecy, souls traded
in the bargain for the prize that evaporates
I have seen this, over & over, living a life
as a fighter, not so much for prizes or cash
just to avoid laying down for a quick payoff
that never looked like it paid much more
than it took back in contingency, if it was
anything at all...so I don't lay down,
                    never fall
                    keep fighting...
        keep fighting until I die

38.

taking the umbilical
preparing it so
gently
drying it
preserving it
in the shape of a heart
so it will never give sustenance
or strangle innocence ever again

39.

Jane goes missing around New Year's Eve
She is the last of the modern primitives
That once roamed the Mesa both little & big
She moves at night through downtowns
Like a eucalyptus bending in a slight wind
on a moonlit night
She is adorned as a tree as she has lost hope
in the ways of man
Her war paint seems placid on her
weathered features
As orange orbs that were once out of season
this time of year
Dangle from her earlobes so gingerly
She stands stoic where cigar stores once
made great plans, banishment for her
Now she smiles inside at the one thing she
knows for certain
That for now, at least, the banishment is on
them
So she disappears from sight every so often
To capture all the meaning every moment
can hold
As we hold our collective breath each time,
waiting hopeful for her return

40.

double down on the twomps
coming at the jugular vein
suck it up hard!   live for it now!

the square root of it comes out even
juice is flowing out everywhere
nothing can stop the flow

nothing but the ferryman, who seems
not to notice for the time being
as the muse hikes her skirt
leaving the money behind, as usual

blindly stumble out into handcuffs
just to be saved by the dawn
like the dawn has never saved you before

41.

never mind this cylinder that spins
nothing in it is as circular as the sphere
this is where we are, in orbit around
each other like a hundred billion atoms
bonded invisibly living life as an illusion
that we are each free particles
never needing each other
 for anything more than
 what we want in selfish moments
 of temporary pleasure fulfillment
or extraordinary entertainment purposes
as we ignore the universal beauty
that is our vast container of love

42.

his art was incessant at 4 a.m.
pounding on the walls, I could feel it,
but, I have to work as well, so I yell 'quiet
down, let the women here sleep, without
your loud artistry crying out to wake us all,
to interrupt our rest we need more than
your art is ever going to be needed by us all
crying out for painful attention, crying out

                                    so loud

43.

clipped wings feed from the bottle
like little dervishes covered in
coastal oil slicks that felt
like love going down
now coming up
with a fearful dilemma
trying to find a lost hope
before it is all too late or ever even on time

44.

suckle up to you
make you feel it
like it is good
then tear your
heart out by
the arteries
just so you
can feel
it pump
one last time

45.

lost valve of love
leave us this last
lonely little life
lived in lustful
loins of longing

46.

there were bluebirds before us
with songs that sing the way
into blissful day dreams
we are not yet
the museum pieces
that collect dust
so readily
we are the cathedral
of hope & suffering
inside the star shaped cactus
looking out on all the crushed planets
that once made this galaxy a home
pinpointing the artery of where we all were
once born forever in a song

47.

Quiet time in the shelter
The children fight
Going to bed
They smile at me
As if nothing is broken
Maybe in that moment
Nothing ever is

48.

our favorite redwood tree fell yesterday
 in a storm
it no longer stands behind the library
 in Big Sur
but, we can never forget the way it stood
above us as we plotted new lives together
underneath the cascade of supernatural
things that invisibly fall on lovers from the
gentle bows of redwood trees that are
slowly dying
in majestic silence along the coastline that
we call home

49.

the locket was never given
a poem that it was promised
until now,
never lost or broken,
never hurt or stolen _ just
                              given
        nothing missing here
          lost or stolen
          hurt or broken
           hearts given
            can never be
             kept that way
                           just
                                given
                                away

50.

Facing judgment
Square in the
Eye
Hearts lose ground
Hope to attain
Wings
Accomplish flight
Escape the gravity
Become
Airborne
Weightless
Like the dreams
Of children
Never knowing
Enough
To quit

...'unitl we meet again, my friend'...

photo by Sean Comstock 2013

This is a writer who believed in the word as a way to be free, no matter the situation. In 2012 he co-founded Punk Hostage Press with Iris Berry. He has traveled the world in his quest to seek peace and understand conflict, mainly his own internal conflict. This has always been his greatest inspiration. On December 25, 1963 he was born in Brooklyn NY. On that same day in 2013 he will be 50 years-old.

He is now living quietly in Point Richmond CA with his greatest love, Naima.

A. Razor Bibliography –

Spare Blades (1985)

Everything Is Shiny Grey (1987)

Evil and Other Safe Lubricants (1989)

Creeping Malaise (1990)

Soaked, Bloated and Waiting to Die (1991)

War in the 13th Hour (1991)

Comp Book (1992)

A Chapbook by A. Razor (1992)

Works (Collected) (1993)

Negative Aspects of a Positive or
(How All the Good can Make All the Bad
Seem even Worse) (1994)

Ash Graffiti After a Riot (1995)

Better Than A Gun In Knife Fight (2012)

Drawn Blood: Collect Works from D.B.P.L.
(2012)

Beaten Up Beaten Down (2012)

Small Catastrophes in a Big World (2012)

Half-Century Status (2013)

Long Winded Tales of a Low Plains Drifter
(2013)